Go to Jerusalem:
A Lenten Devotional

Mary Alice Mulligan

Saint Louis, Missouri

ChalicePress.com

ISBN: 9780827212909

Printed in the United States of America

CONTENTS

Introduction 2

What Does It Mean to Go with Jesus? 4

1st Day of Lent (Ash Wednesday) 4

2d Day of Lent (Thursday) 5

3d Day of Lent (Friday) 6

4th Day of Lent (Saturday) 7

Week 1: Doing What We Know Is Needed 8

5th Day of Lent (Sunday) 8

6th Day of Lent (Monday) 9

7th Day of Lent (Tuesday) 10

8th Day of Lent (Wednesday) 11

9th Day of Lent (Thursday) 12

10th Day of Lent (Friday) 13

11th Day of Lent (Saturday) 14

Week 2: Jesus Our Companion 15

12th Day of Lent (Sunday) 15

13th Day of Lent (Monday) 16

14th Day of Lent (Tuesday) 17

15th Day of Lent (Wednesday) 18

16th Day of Lent (Thursday) 19

17th Day of Lent (Friday) 20

18th Day of Lent (Saturday) 21

Week 3: God Is Worthy of Praise and Worship 22

19th Day of Lent (Sunday) 22
20th Day of Lent (Monday) 23
21st Day of Lent (Tuesday) 24
22d Day of Lent (Wednesday) 25
23d Day of Lent (Thursday) 26
24th Day of Lent (Friday) 27
25th Day of Lent (Saturday) 28

Week 4: Expect New Life 29

26th Day of Lent (Sunday) 29
27th Day of Lent (Monday) 30
28th Day of Lent (Tuesday) 31
29th Day of Lent (Wednesday) 32
30th Day of Lent (Thursday) 33
31st Day of Lent (Friday) 34
32d Day of Lent (Saturday) 35

Week 5: Significant Changes Happen 36

33d Day of Lent (Sunday) 36
34th Day of Lent (Monday) 37
35th Day of Lent (Tuesday) 38
36th Day of Lent (Wednesday) 39
37th Day of Lent (Thursday) 40
38th Day of Lent (Friday) 41
39th Day of Lent (Saturday) 42

Week 6: What About Holy Week? 43

40th Day of Lent (Sunday) 43

41st Day of Lent (Monday) 44

42d Day of Lent (Tuesday) 45

43d Day of Lent (Wednesday) 46

44th Day of Lent (Thursday) 47

45th Day of Lent (Friday) 48

46th Day of Lent (Saturday) 49

47th Day of Lent (Easter Vigil) 50

Reading 48 (Easter Sunday) 51

INTRODUCTION

Dear Readers

Lots of Christians observe the season of Lent every year. Devotional books are created to help Christians learn something new and deepen their faith during a particular period. For Lent this year, Chalice Press encourages you to find a place where you plan to read the devotion each day. Keep a Bible there, too, because we believe for your Lenten devotional journey to strengthen and stretch your faith, you need to take time each day looking up and reading the scripture passage. *Go to Jerusalem* uses both Testaments in the Bible. If you aren't familiar with some of the books, don't be intimidated. You can look up page numbers for them in the front of your Bible. Reading the daily passages can be a special time to be open to what God may be trying to say to you. These devotionals were written using the *New Revised Standard Version*, and the brief excerpts each day are from that translation. You may want to use that translation, or you may prefer to use something else. A different translation is fine, but there may be slight differences in our references to the passages. We hope that makes your experience richer. To assist the process, you will want to get something that will function as a journal so you can keep notes throughout the season. It doesn't have to be fancy. An old spiral notebook will do nicely, or you can start something new. Each day you will want to write in it, responding to the day's questions and writing out the brief prayer that ends the selection. Throughout our weeks together, you should feel encouraged to look back at what you've written in the journal.

As we begin, let me share a story to frame our time together. A friend who is a Dominican friar once told me that each year he has a moment as Lent approaches when he senses Jesus extending his hand and saying, "Michael, let's go to Jerusalem." Some years, Michael puts his hand in Jesus' hand more slowly than other years (after all, the cross is waiting in Jerusalem), but he always finally does, because Jesus is inviting him. Now, we invite you to sense Jesus extending his hand to you and saying, "Beloved disciple, let's go to Jerusalem." Day by day, as we move through Lent, we will travel on the journey with Jesus toward Jerusalem. Each week, we will start with the Sunday gospel reading, and then look at a theme for that week's stretch of the journey. So now, imagine yourself placing your hand in the hand of Jesus for this year's Lenten journey to Jerusalem.

What Does It Mean to Go with Jesus?

1st Day of Lent (Ash Wednesday) Luke 9:51–62

"He set his face to go to Jerusalem."

There is one little sentence less than halfway into the gospel of Luke: Jesus sets his face to go to Jerusalem. Today we might say he made up his mind to go to Jerusalem. It reveals an unyielding determination. So, if our hand stays in his, we will end up in Jerusalem too.

Each of us has reasons for delaying taking his hand. It sounds a little odd to imagine our hand in the hand of someone who lived two thousand years ago. And besides, we expect this Lent to be "same ole same ole." Other daily obligations demand our attention. A devotional is a good discipline, but most of us don't really expect Lent to be life changing. However, the truth is, if we decide to get serious about taking a Lenten journey, we should expect to end up somewhere else. Since we are not boarding a plane for Palestine, our journey will be spiritual. Our time in Bible reading and prayer during Lent might actually take us someplace new in our faith.

In your journal, chronicle some religious change you have gone through: a conversion, a renewed commitment to worship attendance, when you let God help you love your in-laws, or when you became a tither, for instance. Then consider, since God guided you through changes before, that you can grow, mature, change in some way again, if you want to. After you've written your memory, you might copy the prayer below. Then take time to pray it.

Prayer: *Inviting Companion, I have no idea where this journey may take us, but I will try to trust that once I put my hand in yours, you will never let me go. Lead me where you will. Amen.*

2[d] Day of Lent (Thursday) Isaiah 55:6–13

"So shall my word be that goes out from my mouth; it shall not return to me empty."

Different seasons of the year serve different purposes. The glorious colors and fragrances of early flowers exploding in many areas right now last just a brief time, but the season is crucial for plants to bear the fruit and seeds that lead to reproduction. The days of rain many of us experience in spring are crucial for replenishing the land. God's plans for Earth follow God's guidance, to make sure there is abundant life, season after season.

God's scriptural word also bears fruit, season after season, in our lives. Sometimes we need to hear basic tenets of the faith, so we read Acts 2. Other times we might need to push ourselves deeper toward spiritual maturity, so we read the Sermon on the Mount in Matthew 5–7. Or we might need comfort, so we read John 14. No matter what part of God's word we listen to, we are assured it will not return empty. We are always fed and watered by scripture and by sharing with others how we believe God is working among us, so scripture helps us stay close to Jesus on our journey to Jerusalem.

In your journal, can you record a time you were nourished by scripture or by someone's sharing words from God with you? It would be a good idea to commit yourself to reading the proposed scripture each day. Can you write how God's purposes are being carried out as you receive God's word? Is there someone you might share a word with today?

***Prayer**: God of every season, thank you for feeding my soul, season after season, my whole life long. Amen.*

3d Day of Lent (Friday) Romans 12:1–2

"Present your bodies as a living sacrifice."

Did you ever notice how some people are just sure their trip is going to be a disaster and others are just as sure their trip is going to be a magnificent experience? You can hear them in line at the airport or as you pay for gas at the station on the highway. "I'm so afraid that..." or "I'm so excited that..." And most of the time, each of them is correct. Someone once said, "In life, you get what you expect." Of course, this isn't always true, but especially on a spiritual journey, preparing for an important experience sets the stage for it. So, what will you do to prepare? Remember the image of placing your hand in the hand of Jesus as the journey of Lent began? Romans 12 invites us to put our whole selves into Jesus' hands. Can you imagine it? Of course, God doesn't have body parts, but you can sense the experience nonetheless. Holy outstretched hands, ready to receive everything you are. All of your weaknesses, all of your frustrations, all of your good intentions, even your physical weaknesses and strengths—you are invited to turn them over to God. And when you pour everything into God's care, all that you are becomes holy and acceptable to God. You are a holy sacrifice and this is your spiritual worship.

In your journal, note how it feels to rest in God's holy presence. Your comfort and your joy in God's acceptance are worship, pleasing to God.

Prayer: *With the confidence of a child, I rest in your supportive arms, heavenly Parent. Amen.*

4th Day of Lent (Saturday) Psalm 73:21–26

"You hold my right hand."

If we get honest, none of us faithfully follows Jesus Christ every minute of every day, no matter how hard we try. Even Sunday school teachers and church prayer warriors falter at times. Everyone gets distracted; we get careless. However, we have chosen to take this journey with Jesus, imperfect as we are, ready to end up in a new place. So what does it mean to go with Jesus? First, it means being open to God's lead. The journey is spiritual, so we must trust God's guidance. This psalm reminds us of one thing that will help us, flawed humans that we are: desire. We need to desire God. So, we check ourselves. As we commit to this journey, can we again place our hand in Jesus' outstretched hand because we trust his counsel? Can we believe that whenever we falter, the Holy Spirit is always ready to help us regain our balance and guide us back onto the path? Do we desire closeness with God?

In your journal, consider your own level of trust in God's ability to accompany you on the journey. Do you trust Jesus, even if the path is taking you someplace unknown? Can you stir up your own desire for God's presence in your life? If so, write a thanksgiving to God. But if you feel spiritually dry or even empty right now, write about those feelings, confident that your willingness to keep reaching out to God will result in eventually sensing God's strengthening presence. You are not abandoned.

Prayer: *Merciful Savior, you are my heart's desire. When I wander away from you, please draw me back into your care. Thank you. Amen.*

Week 1: Doing What We Know Is Needed

5th Day of Lent (Sunday) Mark 1:9–15

"In those days Jesus came from Nazareth of Galilee and was baptized by John."

This week we investigate what is needed on our Lenten journey. Why should we start with the baptism of Jesus? Baptism is for repentance and forgiveness of sin. Why would Jesus need baptism? The truth is Jesus doesn't need baptism; he chooses to be baptized. If Jesus is the word of God incarnate, he exists physically. He is flesh and blood, a real person. His body needs food, rest, companionship. As Jesus participates in life activities, he isn't God pretending to be human. He is God incarnate as a fully human person. He enters the water of baptism for the same reason he entered the world: to be with us. To be one of us.

At Jesus' baptism, the barrier between earth and heaven is divinely ripped open. God claims the beloved sonship of the one baptized. A new era begins for Jesus, who is then driven into the wilderness, the place of spiritual contemplation, temptation, and struggle. These experiences of water and wilderness mark the beginning of his true ministry of upside-down teachings, flouting social restrictions, and declaring unconditional grace.

Can you make a list of what Jesus' life was like before his baptism? What rules did he follow and what did he learn? And then can you list changes? Note the people he now touches, the new teachings he begins to claim, the spiritual power at his disposal. In thinking about the changes in his life, consider—how did baptism change your life?

Prayer: *Like each of us, blessed Jesus of Nazareth, someone taught you to walk and talk, taught you the faith. Help me understand the dramatic changes you went through as you were baptized and took time preparing for your future. Amen.*

6th Day of Lent (Monday) Psalm 51:1–17

"Create in me a clean heart, O God."

Many people mark the beginning of Lent using this scripture, meditating on it on Ash Wednesday. As we head into our first full week of Lent, this scripture reminds us sharply that we cannot be holy on our own, no matter how hard we try. When we look at ourselves honestly, our sins are quite obvious. We know we do things we shouldn't; we ignore things we need to take care of; we neglect to share our abundance with those in need; we pretend we are better persons than we are. The truth is we cannot get much better on our own. What do we need as we head toward Jerusalem? We need to get honest. We need a broken and contrite heart. We need God. If our transgressions are to be blotted out, it will only be by the mercy of God. Lent gives us the opportunity to admit that God already sees fully into our hearts, into the truth of our being. Only when we acknowledge our need for God are we able to rejoice in the grace extended to us. Holy forgiveness cleanses us and promises to create a clean heart within us. Don't we all need that?

As you contemplate your life during this season of Lent, answer these questions in your journal: What would your clean heart look like? What would be different in your life, your actions, your attitude? Would anyone be able to tell? How?

Prayer: *You alone, merciful Savior, can put a new and right spirit within me. Have your way. Amen.*

7th Day of Lent (Tuesday) Matthew 4:1–11

"Then Jesus was led up by the Spirit into the wilderness to be tempted."

Matthew's account of Jesus' baptism adds details Mark's does not. Take a few minutes to remember your own baptism or baptisms you have witnessed. Baptism is an important step on each Christian's faith journey. Like many of us, Jesus made the decision to be baptized, but then immediately afterwards, temptations were stirred up. We may not be able to fast for forty days, but some of us know the feeling of participating in some spiritual discipline, even experiencing a spiritual high from it, which can be a wonderful sensation. But then, almost predictably, some crisis knocks us to the ground or some temptation lures us away. Suddenly we are once again weak and vulnerable. The temptations Jesus faced are fairly familiar. We all crave power to get what we want, like lush possessions or protection from danger. But in his answers, Jesus shows us what we need. Meditating on scripture can ward off temptations and remind us that God's power trumps evil.

Can you get honest with yourself to write down what you do when you are threatened by temptation? How do you thwart evil? Can you tell when such experiences are starting and counteract them early? Do you have a trusted friend who can help you stay strong? If you don't have one, how would you go about finding one? Noting in your journal when you are successful in warding off temptations can be a good way to encourage yourself in the future when you reread your writings.

Prayer: *Blessed Son of God, you strengthen and guide me when temptations arise. Please continue to help me avoid giving in to my weaknesses. I need you on my daily journey. Amen.*

8th Day of Lent (Wednesday)

Acts 16:25–35

"Believe on the Lord Jesus, and you will be saved."

In the sixteenth century, some European Christians killed other European Christians over an interpretation of this passage. They claimed since the jailer's household would have included babies, the practice of infant baptism is scriptural. Believers who limited baptism only to immersion, they argued, were acting against scripture. Others claim the passage is not explicit about infants, whereas other New Testament depictions of baptisms are clearly limited to those who could ask for it. Arguing over the practice of infant baptism misses an important focus of the passage. The Philippian jailer's question is one most of us have asked: What must I do to be saved? Paul shares the great news. Believe God's presence has come to earth in Jesus' flesh to set loose God's saving power in the world. Believe Jesus' teachings will guide you to a life of discernment and joy. Believe that God acts in every baptism, granting people the Holy Spirit's empowerment. Believe your fellow believers will join you in worship and service and rejoicing.

Are those the statements you would use to tell someone the good news? If not, feel free to write out statements you think are more fitting. How do you explain your belief in Jesus? Describe how your beliefs have changed your life. Can you think of someone who needs to hear how much God loves them? Even if it's scary, can you figure out a way to approach them?

Prayer: *You set me free from my past, Holy Ground of Release. Deepen my belief, that I may know the joy of my salvation. Amen.*

9th Day of Lent (Thursday) Isaiah 58:1–12

"You shall be called the repairer of the breach, the restorer of streets to live in."

In one church, the sanctuary was open on Ash Wednesday for people to come in for meditation, prayer, and personal Bible reading. The minister was present throughout the day to offer additional prayer and blessing and to make the sign of the cross in ashes on their forehead if requested. One worshipper found herself alone with the pastor, so she talked about her theology, her faith, and her appreciation for how their congregation allowed for a variety of theological and social justice positions, yet they stayed together. She concluded, "We each need a congregation." We really cannot be faithful followers of Jesus without a community of believers supporting, challenging, and worshipping with us. Isaiah warns against going through communal rituals without paying attention to God's desires for Earth's people. We are not just to perform certain behaviors to please God. Our behaviors should further God's purposes: correcting injustices, making sure all people have enough of life's necessities, eliminating oppression. When we participate in these actions, God is pleased. We are mending the world's breaches.

Think of a way your congregation has shined God's light through its actions. Write about that experience in your journal. Has your congregation ever served as a restorer of streets to live in? Record that. Can you see places in the world where holy mending is needed? How might you help your congregation move forward to be a repairer of the breach, a healer of brokenness, a bringer of justice?

Prayer: *Guide us, LORD Yahweh, to bring your purposes to fruition on Earth. Amen.*

10th Day of Lent (Friday) Matthew 18:15–20

"Let such a one be to you as a Gentile and a tax collector."

Let us note it again. Our faith journey requires a faith community. We need each other. Although no congregation is perfect, these teachings of Jesus give guidance to local churches. The big idea isn't rules for settling every argument, but guidance that as a community of faith, we need to be honest about how certain behaviors affect others. Someone needs to point out that it is silly to let our feelings get hurt over someone else's cutting the pies at the potluck. We also need others to point out that we are wrong to refuse to release funds for a project we do not like. And sometimes we must confront sin among us. In a congregation of varied members, each with different gifts and talents tucked within them by the Holy Spirit, disagreements happen, but we are empowered to reach compromises and share responsibilities. And when someone refuses to listen, Jesus' directions to treat them as a tax collector or Gentile does not mean to cut them off. Look how Jesus treats tax collectors. He asks to sit down to a meal with them. He invites them into God's presence. When barriers arise in our fellowship, perhaps after a little cooling off period, we might try having a meal together, not to reach a compromise about the issue, but to reconnect in friendship through Jesus Christ.

Can you describe a situation you need to work on? In your journal, can you spell out some options for dealing with it?

Prayer: *Firm Giver of guidance, you believe we can heal any wounds in our fellowship. Help us believe it too. Amen.*

11th Day of Lent (Saturday) Psalm 32

"While I kept silence, my body wasted away."

Every one of us is an imperfect Christian. The truth is each of us sins in our Christian walk. What continues to hurt us after sinning is the silence we often keep as a result. Our shame can block our being honest with God or with anyone else, so the weight of it continues to burden us. But if we get honest, confess before God whatever is going on in our life, forgiveness is assured. Admitting what we have done and sensing divine grace is a tremendous relief. The psalmist tells us that as a result we will find shelter, a hiding place, in God's presence. God becomes our refuge.

Have you ever felt so bad you couldn't even tell God about it? Maybe you have some incident you still need to confess. Lent is a great time to get clear. Sometimes writing down what we want to say is an easier way to articulate it. For most of us, writing our failings down is very difficult. But it can be tremendously healing. Can you remember a former action you asked God to forgive? Do you remember the sense of peace you felt after you confessed and believed God forgave you? Maybe your situation isn't what you did but what happened to you. Silence about some hurt can also burden us. Can you put it into words in your journal, asking God to help you heal? Can you, even now, feel God's sheltering presence surrounding you?

Prayer: *Gracious Holy One, thank you for lifting me from my shame and forgiving me. Thank you for embracing me in your grace. Amen.*

Week 2: Jesus Our Companion

12th Day of Lent (Sunday) Mark 8:31–38

"If any want to become my followers, let them ... take up their cross and follow me."

How comforting to consider Jesus as our closest companion. Whatever mess we wander into, he is there to help us out of it. But as our faith matures, we realize asking Jesus to go where we have planned to go is inappropriate. Instead, we should listen to him and follow. Peter declares Jesus to be Messiah, but when Jesus begins unpacking what that means, Peter rebukes him. Rudely he attempts to correct the one he just declared is Christ. Naturally, Peter doesn't like what he hears. Neither will we if we actually listen. Our Savior predicts his own rejection, torturous suffering, and execution, but also his resurrection. Then, Jesus flatly tells his followers to expect the same for themselves. We must pick up a cross and go where Jesus goes. This is quite different from holding hands with Jesus and assuming he will follow us through our day. He calls us to a life of sacrifice and compassion. Just as he boldly proclaimed God's love for the rejected, and included the socially unacceptable as his closest friends, so Jesus calls us to live differently. We must commit all that we are and all that we have to going where Jesus sends us. He might lead us to sew school uniforms for children in another country, or double our mission giving, or pack weekend food backpacks for local school children, or visit a nursing home, or adopt a child. When our hand is correctly in Jesus' hand, he leads and we follow him.

Prayer: *It sounds awful, Human One, to go through what you predict, so please strengthen me to be able to follow. Amen.*

13th Day of Lent (Monday)

Mark 6:30–32

"Come away to a deserted place all by yourselves and rest a while."

Earlier in this chapter, Jesus sends out the disciples to teach and heal. Then we hear about the beheading of John the Baptizer. Without any kind of a break, the disciples return to Jesus, effervescing with the success of all they have done and taught. Jesus encourages them to "come away," taking them to an isolated place to rest. What a wonderful little break. Jesus knows that after dramatic new responsibilities anyone needs time to rejuvenate. Even we need rest if we have been stretching our faith life. When Jesus calls us to a new task, he also expects us to find time and place to rest.

Marilyn, a new mission coworker, was "on fire for the Lord" when she was sent to serve in Mexico. She had almost no discretionary income, so her diet every day was what people donated: rice and beans, something she had never eaten much in her previous life. Week after week, she ate a monotonous diet of rice and beans. Then one day, a pickup truck arrived at her trailer. The driver called out, "I don't have any money to give to the mission, but I have some day-old bread and a few jars of peanut butter. I think God wanted me to bring them here." It was as if Jesus had called her to come away and rest. Feast on her favorite food, peanut butter sandwiches.

Are you a person who neglects taking care of yourself? Can you write about a time Jesus led you to rest?

Prayer: *Welcoming Guide, thank you for providing nourishment for our hungry bodies and rest when our new tasks make our souls weary. Amen.*

14th Day of Lent (Tuesday)

John 4:46–54

"The man believed the word that Jesus spoke to him."

Don't we all want miraculous signs and wonders from God? We may laugh at those who believe God protects them so they can safely take up snakes, but deep inside we want God to perform miracles around us. Even peanut butter when we're tired of rice and beans. Some people are struggling to have a baby, or wondering where the money will come from for next month's bills, or caring for a parent with baffling needs, or waiting for a diagnosis from unclear test results. In the midst of world events, our lives keep happening. No wonder sometimes we feel the need for a miracle. But most of us will not receive a long-distance healing, as the child in the scripture did. So how do we keep the faith? I think we choose to keep going in spite of the circumstances. We choose to keep believing that Jesus is present with us, even when the signs and wonders don't appear. We wake up in the morning and we say, "Today, I choose you, Jesus, to be my Savior, no matter what else happens." And if we pay attention, there is a miracle. We discover we have faith in the midst of our doubt or troubles. We have the faith to keep on trusting God's presence and grace. We have the strength to keep going.

Write out your own faith commitment. It doesn't have to sound perfect. Describe how today you choose to believe in Jesus as your Savior.

Prayer: *Ever-present Companion, I do choose you today. Help me sense your presence surrounding me, guiding and strengthening me, no matter what. Amen.*

15th Day of Lent (Wednesday)

Isaiah 42:1–9

"I have taken you by the hand and kept you."

The prophets who wrote the book of Isaiah had no idea that more than a millennium later some people would interpret their description of the Suffering Servant to mean an itinerant Galilean rabbi. But many identify Jesus with the servant upon whom God has placed the Holy Spirit and who has been directed to bring justice to Earth. What is more profitable is to note that the servant points to God's desire for the world to be different through God's power to bring about change. The servant accomplishes God's desires by doing what servants do. They serve. The servant here is to bring about justice and righteousness, open blind eyes, and set prisoners free. In other words, to work in the world to set things straight, releasing the oppressed, assisting the poor and struggling, and creating a just society. The prophets are intentionally vague in describing the servant, perhaps as a reminder that just as the servant points to God and serves God's purposes, so should those who follow the servant or attempt to be servants of God point to God and serve God's purposes in the world.

If Jesus is Servant of God, you are his servant. How have you been a servant of the Servant? Have you worked to help establish justice? Have you sensed God calling you to righteousness and taking you by the hand?

Prayer: *Holy LORD Yahweh, help me follow the Servant you have called. Amen.*

16th Day of Lent (Thursday)

John 10:1–10

"Very truly, I tell you, I am the gate for the sheep."

Twice in these brief verses Jesus uses his powerful "I AM" statement, connecting his actions with the divine name revealed to Moses centuries before at the burning bush: "I am who I am" (Yahweh) (Exodus 3:14). When he says, "I am the gate," he is claiming divine identity. And by the way, Jesus simultaneously calls us his sheep: silly, practically brainless sheep, although we are able to identify the shepherd's voice. Jesus calls us to enter a life of safety and wholeness through him. He speaks in the present tense to explain to us that salvation is not only about spending eternity with God. We are invited to experience a life of true abundance now. The gate leads to salvation—that is, Jesus is claiming that entering by the gate saves us from a life of ongoing emptiness and irrelevance. We aren't promised luxury, but salvation through Jesus means finding holy meaning and purpose for our life now.

Can you think of ways Jesus has been a Gate for a better life for you? Write about them. Has he helped you find meaning and purpose? In what ways? Do you know someone who needs to hear about Jesus as a gate to wholeness? It may not be someone who is a drunkard or a rabble-rouser; sometimes it's someone who just doesn't know life can have meaning or hope. Could you pluck up courage to talk with them about how Christ is the way into a life of purpose?

Prayer: *Blessed Gate of salvation, call my name, hold my hand, and lead me where you want me to be. Amen.*

17th Day of Lent (Friday) 1 Timothy 1:12–17

"The grace of our Lord overflowed for me with the faith and love that are in Christ Jesus."

All week we have considered the companionship of Christ on our journey to Jerusalem. Most of us are painfully aware that our lives are not the glowing examples of faithfulness we wish they were. Each of us has cringeworthy periods in our past—for some of us, a not-so-distant past. Why would Jesus want to travel with us? However, as we acknowledge that he does want to be with us, consider the amazing corollary to our shameful pasts. The writer of this letter states it bluntly: "Christ Jesus came into the world to save sinners." Glorious words! God became incarnate because of our deep need. The writer claims to have been dramatically changed—saved—by Christ Jesus. For him, it meant moving from ignorance to knowledge, from separation from God to connection with God's plans, from guilt to forgiveness.

As you and Jesus travel together, try to put into words what you have been saved from. Write it down. How have you been changed in the life you are now living? What does salvation mean in this current period of your life? Have you been set free in some way? Take time to put into words what believing in Jesus has done in your life. You may need to think about it throughout the day and write about it this evening. And then take time to thank Jesus Christ for saving you. In addition to the prayer below, you might want to write out your own prayer.

Prayer: *To the Monarch of the ages, immortal, invisible, the only God, be honor and glory forever and ever. Amen.*

18th Day of Lent (Saturday) Matthew 28:16–20

"Make disciples of all nations."

Each of the four gospels and the book of Acts record different final scenes following the resurrection of Jesus. With all their varied descriptions, they cannot be reconciled into one narrative, which shows us the writers were not giving exact reports of historical events but faith meanings for the nascent church to comprehend. Notice that one overriding idea is consistent. The resurrected Christ always points believers into the future together, with hope. We are to move forward as a group. Jesus is not only a companion for our individual journey; he creates us to be a church community, promising we do not move forward alone. He promises to be with us. In another gospel, he breathes the Holy Spirit onto his followers. Even in the briefest ending in Mark, the angel sends the women to get the disciples to join them in Galilee, where Jesus will meet them. None of us has to figure out how to walk with Jesus alone. The faith community has the guidance of the Spirit of Jesus to help us mature, stretch, and grow as followers of Jesus Christ. Jesus' plan is the church.

Can you think of a time the church offered you guidance for your life, which you now realize was from God? Have you ever helped your congregation work through a difficult decision or issue? Did you sense the presence of God in the process, as your congregation worked? Take time to record these experiences and where you sensed God working with you.

Prayer: *Spirit of the Living Christ, we praise you. Continue to fill your church with wisdom and power. Use us to spread your word of love throughout the world. Amen.*

Week 3: God Is Worthy of Praise and Worship

19th Day of Lent (Sunday) John 2:13–22

"Stop making my Father's house a marketplace!"

Jesus' ministry is absolutely grounded in the belief that God is worthy of praise and worship. Jesus drives out those who made the temple a marketplace, who ignore that it is his Father's house. So, does it make you shudder to imagine Jesus storming your Sunday morning service shouting that everyone should "get out!" because none of the worshippers is focused on the holiness of God? Can you imagine him laying out the truth that too many of us focus on the latest news or carrying out church tasks? As we move toward the middle of Lent, let's take a serious look in the mirror. We sing that God is the center of our lives, our joy and strength. We say God's love gives us life, and we promise to respond in love. But if family comes into town, we comfortably use them as an excuse not to get to worship that day. Or if this is the one perfect Sunday all spring for a golf game or planting the garden or visiting a relative, we have no problem skipping. Such behavior indicates God is worthy of worship—unless something else comes up. Shouldn't worship take priority?

You might record in your journal why God is worthy of worship. Why is worshipping with a faith community important? Does it help you understand the faith better? Does it reflect your commitment to scripture, which calls us to worship? Does something happen when we sing praises, offer financial gifts, and pray together? What?

Prayer: *Eternal God, forgive me when I neglect to praise you, for surely you are worthy. Amen.*

20th Day of Lent (Monday)

Jeremiah 8:18–22

"For the hurt of my poor people I am hurt."

"Jeremiad," meaning a long, mournful lament, comes from the book of Jeremiah. Here, God is agonizing over the people's pain, which they caused themselves. Clearly God's heart is breaking over their distress. Of course, everyone experiences pain throughout their life. Sometimes hurt passes quickly and we rejoice, like when a child recovers from illness. But sometimes the pain seems endless. How can one just expect to "get over" the death of a spouse, the betrayal of a close friend, or a con artist stealing one's retirement savings? We know the child's recovery was not because we prayed correctly and God performed a miracle for us. God does not kill some people and save others. We also know our ongoing suffering from a death, betrayal, or conniving theft is not divine punishment because we prayed wrong, even though it sometimes feels that way. Diseases, accidents, and chance act in our lives, but God does not punish us with them. We know it, even when our suffering goes on and on without relief. So we rightly call out to God, knowing that although God does not solve our pain, God aches with us. God moans with us.

Have you experienced a painful situation when prayer seemed futile? Can you articulate your feelings? Does it help to remember God is listening and hurts with you? Can you chronicle what you think God would like to say to you? Do you know someone going through a time of long suffering? Can you listen and hurt with them?

Prayer: *For times I have not been hurting, I give you thanks, most compassionate God. And for times I struggle to be saved from pain, help me know your presence. Amen.*

21st Day of Lent (Tuesday) Romans 15:5–13

"So that together you may with one voice glorify the God and Father of our Lord Jesus Christ."

One New Testament scholar claims Romans 15:7 is the key to the entire letter. If we treat each other as Christ treats us, God is glorified. Paul writes to teach us how to be church, the body of Christ on Earth. And what is the church for? Certainly it is for teaching the faith and welcoming those who haven't heard the good news of God's love revealed in the life, ministry, death, and resurrection of Jesus Christ. And church is also a conduit for service. As a community of faith, we provide energy for outreach projects; supplies when disasters hit; and financial support for ministry going on in our neighborhoods and around the world. But the most important function of church is worship. We gather to offer God praise and thanksgiving because God is worthy. The One who is the source of life, who forgives whatever unforgivable acts we perform, and who, scripture tells us, is love itself—that One is worthy of all honor and glory, all adoration and devotion. Worshipping together glorifies God and shapes us into the church God deserves.

Take some time to consider what church means to you. Can you write about how church should help you focus on how God deserves your worship? Write about a time you sensed you were worshipping God in your congregation. What was different from times you did not sense much worship going on? Were you different on those occasions, or was something different in the service, or both?

Prayer: *May the God of steadfastness and encouragement grant you to live in harmony with one another, in accordance with Christ Jesus, so that together you may with one voice glorify the God and Father of our Lord Jesus Christ. Amen.*

22d Day of Lent (Wednesday)

Isaiah 43:15–21

"For I give water in the wilderness, rivers in the desert, to give drink to my chosen people, the people whom I formed for myself so that they might declare my praise."

This passage touches some of our deepest emotions. The people were dragged into exile and now are stricken with wrenching discouragement, so Yahweh helps them recall their escape from Egyptian enslavement centuries earlier. That exodus saved the Hebrews from lives of endless, meaningless servitude. Now, centuries later in exile, a downcast Judah is reminded that God can make a way out of no way. God replenishes their lagging souls with promises of a real future. Such hope provides sustenance for their starving spirits. During the weeks of Covid-19 self-isolation, many people felt as if they were in exile. Normal activities were halted. Usual contacts were prohibited. Even now, we aren't completely confident in our steps toward normality.

Can you write about how God provided water in some wilderness time you experienced over the past year? What person or resources did God use? Can you remember another time when God made a way out for you? Write about it. Do you feel like you are in exile now? If so, do you trust God's presence with you? And do you believe this exile is temporary? How might you thank God right now for the release you know is coming? If you do not feel like you are in exile, do you know someone else who might feel isolated and vulnerable now? Can you bring a word of hope and future to them? You might ask them how God rescued them from some past experience.

Prayer: *Ruler of history, there have always been times of crisis and times of ease. Help me trust your future. Amen.*

23d Day of Lent (Thursday) Mark 7:1–8

"In vain do they worship me."

I have a distinct memory of my mother listening attentively as I gave a detailed, scene-by-scene description of a movie I saw one afternoon. She probably could not have cared less about the movie, but it meant a great deal to me that she listened. Years later, I have forgotten the movie, but I remember my mother's attention to something I cared about. When someone pays attention to us, we notice. This passage from Mark shows how God notices when we pay attention. Is a religious ritual important, or is it mindlessly performed, like brushing our teeth before going to bed? God yearns for our attention, for our hearts to be reaching out to God in worship.

Do you ever wonder whether God is saddened by times we half attend to worship? Do you ever catch yourself singing hymns completely oblivious to what the words say? Does your mind wander during prayer time? Instead of beating yourself up for not being fully present in worship, maybe you can just figure out ways to keep your focus. One way is to prepare for worship before leaving home. Take time to notice where you are going. Then open yourself to God's infinite presence; sense God's love surrounding you as you travel toward your church worship space. Arrive early enough to sit quietly in preparation, thanking God for bringing you through another week. Then as worship begins, focus on how God is worthy of worship. In your journal, write how you will prepare for worship this week.

Prayer: *Cleanse my thoughts, my heart, and my mind, that I may be prepared to worship you fully, most worthy God. Amen.*

24th Day of Lent (Friday)

Psalm 71:1–12

"Be to me a rock of refuge."

Every year, the Lenten season invites us to be attentive to our spiritual life, but the One who first thought of us has been closer than our own breath our whole lives. Whenever we want, we can throw ourselves into God's arms in prayer and share our deepest joys and pains, knowing that God understands more than our words are able to babble out. Although we may sometimes feel distant from God, we never are. God is like a pesky little sister who tags after us no matter what. We may feel we've gotten away from her, but if we just turn around, there she is. God is never absent, never absentminded. When times are difficult for us, if we pay attention, we'll notice that God is most persistently present. We are frail flesh, as Lent emphasizes, yet God is our present hope, our strength, and our protection. God is always leaning toward us.

Can you take a moment to revel in the glorious, constant presence of God? Remember that you put your hand in Jesus' hand for this journey. He will hold you. Can you offer thankful praise for God's ongoing gifts of life and love and forgiveness? Are there times you felt distant from God? How did it change? Write down what changed and how. Now take a few minutes to consider others. Do you know someone who may need to be reminded that God is always present in their life? Could you reach out and offer to pray with them?

Prayer: *Ever-present Refuge, when I am weak and discouraged, help me sense your power drawing me closer to your love. Amen.*

25th Day of Lent (Saturday) Revelation 4:1–11

"Day and night without ceasing they sing, 'Holy, holy, holy'."

The Disney movie *Fantasia* uses the musical composition "Night on Bald Mountain" to underscore a heart-pounding scene of a mountainous, sinister figure drawing souls from graves as "all hell breaks loose." Souls dance and writhe in pain as fire envelops them until dawn. Then, "Ave Maria" begins a gentle procession of lighted souls heading to paradise. "Bald Mountain" is exciting. The lighted procession is relaxing, but it can easily get old. Preachers know sin is always easier to describe than salvation. Revelation's image of heavenly creatures falling facedown before the throne of God in praise raises our curiosity, but it is difficult to imagine our interest being held there for long. However, if we open ourselves to the magnificent goodness of God, we might actually understand the attraction of eternal worship. When people first fall in love, they endlessly bask in the pleasure of each other's presence. Parents stare in awe at the miracle of a sleeping newborn. Hours can pass without them noticing time at all. Maybe the "Ave Maria" artists were sadly just not very imaginative. Focusing on God should result, as Charles Wesley notes in the hymn "Love Divine, All Loves Excelling," in our becoming "lost in wonder, love, and praise."

Can you write reasons for worship, reactions to God's goodness and love? Have you received God's mercy? Think of the glory of creation. Can you thank God for the crocuses that indefatigably push up every spring, even when a late freeze comes? Have you heard a bird sing today? Did you see the sun or listen to the rain today? Are the days getting longer?

Prayer: *Blessing and glory and wisdom and thanksgiving and honor and power and might be to our God forever and ever! Amen.*

Week 4: Expect New Life

26th Day of Lent (Sunday)

John 3:14–21

"Indeed, God did not send the Son into the world to condemn the world."

Signs used to appear frequently in ballparks: John 3:16. This one verse was used to draw a line in the dirt. On one side, people who believe in Jesus will go to heaven. On the other side, those who don't will go to hell. What the signs really meant was "believe in Jesus the same way I do, or too bad for you." The focus seemed to be getting people to their side of a line in the dirt. But the gospel says Jesus is to save the whole world. So what does that mean? Curiously, the judgment statements may help explain salvation best. Those who do not believe in Jesus are condemned (or judged) already. There is no indication John means an afterlife punishment, but rather that those who do not "get" who Jesus is are already stumbling around in the dark. Those who are working to figure out Jesus are already living into the reality God plans for the whole world. Someone in the twenty-first century might say that salvation involves a world paradigm shift, a total change of perspective, as if being born into reality as God intends it.

Can you write about times you acted as if you forgot to turn on God's lights—perhaps a time you acted meanly or selfishly, hoping no one would find out? And can you also note times you behaved in ways that expressed love for God and others? Did you ever feel like new life was breaking in because of your belief in Jesus?

Prayer: *Beloved Savior, open my eyes and teach me your ways. Amen.*

27th Day of Lent (Monday) Matthew 19:23–26

"Then who can be saved?"

If our focus this week is on expecting new life, we should remember change is not easy. If there is new life, something old probably has to go. Jesus talks about money and possessions more than he talks about anything else, so let's think what "new life" means for those of us who, in the eyes of the world, are "rich" (meaning we have more than enough to meet basic needs). Someone—it may have been Christian ethicist William Stringfellow—wrote that a camel can go through the eye of a needle but will be unrecognizable when it comes out the other side. For a rich person to free herself from wealth involves a similarly dramatic change. Her "new life" on the other side may be almost impossible to recognize. No wonder Jesus says it's impossible for us to do it on our own. Who would want to?

Think of your own wealth compared to the one in five people on Earth who is desperately poor. Do you have any kind of a nest egg? Did you ever take a vacation? Does dinner every night fill you? And do you expect breakfast? Write in your journal how you might free yourself from some of your wealth. Get specific. Even if it seems like you don't have much, what might you do without? Can you imagine living without those things if it meant being clearer about your faith? Might you actually draw closer to Jesus if you had fewer things and less money?

Prayer: *Rabbi Jesus, many nights you had no roof and no comfortable place to lay your head. We never hear of your having fancy clothes or possessions. Help me think about what you might like me to do without. Amen.*

28th Day of Lent (Tuesday) 2 Chronicles 36:15–23

(Make sure you read to the end.)

"Let him go up."

When the people of Judah were defeated by a foreign army, the unimaginable happened. Jerusalem fell. LORD Yahweh's temple was destroyed. How could God's house be conquered and plundered? A stunned people were hauled off into exile in Babylon. Only peasants and old people were left behind in Judah. They would certainly not be mounting a rescue of the exiles. And the Babylonians were so powerful, the exiled people could never organize a successful rebellion against them. Judah was clearly doomed to endless servanthood in Babylon. They must have felt God had abandoned them and that they would never be free. For seventy years they lived with that reality: There is no remedy.

But salvation did come, from the most unbelievable place. When Persia, the mightiest monarchy, arose, conquering even Babylon, the Persian king Cyrus is said to have allowed any exiled people of Judah to return to Jerusalem and rebuild the temple. No one, absolutely no one, would have predicted release coming from another conquest, yet God is able to take any circumstance and bring meaningful life from it.

Can you think of a time you found new meaning or life or rescue from a totally unpredictable place? Take time to find a memory and write about it. Can you discover how God may have been at work in it? Does this give you hope for some circumstance in your life today? Can you construct words of thankfulness to God for the new meaning or rescue you don't even see coming?

Prayer: *LORD God, Holy One, thank you for continuing to work in all the circumstances of my life. Help me watch for your actions around me. Amen.*

29th Day of Lent (Wednesday) Luke 10:1–12

"Like lambs into the midst of wolves."

For people who did not grow up in the church, it is difficult to know what to expect when the teachings of Jesus first begin to matter to them. It is a little like being invited to a friend's house on your birthday. You expect something is about to happen, but you cannot guess what. A large group of disciples had followed Jesus for quite some time, but then he sent them out in pairs on their own while he stayed behind. They must have been excited, terrified, befuddled. What do you think? Jesus sends them out like lambs among wolves to prepare people for his arrival. They are allowed no provisions. How could they possibly know what to expect? And yet they go. This is an important lesson for us too. They go where directed because they trust that Jesus would not send them out in vain. They return (Luke 10:17) with joy at their success.

In your journal, reflect on some moment in your faith journey when you stepped out into new territory because you sensed God directing you. How scary was that? Are you glad you went? Consider where you are in your current journey. Look back in your journal. Might Jesus be guiding you to step out again? Might new life be coming from such a move? Where might you find a prayer partner to share the possibility of moving into new territory in your faith? Are you bold enough to ask someone to pray with you every week?

Prayer: *Ever-patient Guide, calm my timidity and strengthen me to take new steps in my faith, so I may find new richness in my relationship with you. Amen.*

30th Day of Lent (Thursday) Ephesians 3:14–21

"That Christ may dwell in your hearts through faith, as you are being rooted and grounded in love."

Every local church is a living, growing organism, which means we are changing. Our congregations grow older or larger or smaller; some grow in faith, while others grow weary. Each of the various ways we grow means we must learn new ways to be church. Fortunately, God guides our path to new life, even when we are dragging our heels because we don't think we will like the changes that result. And the Spirit of Christ strengthens us together as church as we find our way. Paul's line that we are being rooted and grounded in love reminds me of the crepe myrtle in my front yard that kept putting up shoots from the ground. I cut them off so the tree would look less shaggy. I stuck them in water, hoping they would root. They did not. But I stuck those bare sticks in a pot of dirt and moved them to my new home. You guessed it—little green buds popped out on three of the sticks. New life from something that appeared dead. When we are planted in sacred love, new life is assured.

Think of some new life that happened in your church. Maybe the music program changed, or a group of different people joined, or new ways of communication were established, or people who never led committees before were elected. Did you resist change at first? How did you come to embrace it? Where is God in congregational change? What does new life look like now?

Prayer: *Thank you, guiding Holy One, for bringing me to this congregation and for the faithful journey we are taking together. Amen.*

31st Day of Lent (Friday) John 15:12–17

"I am giving you these commands so that you may love one another."

Our Lenten journey offers opportunities to draw closer to Jesus, to deepen our spiritual life, and to connect in new ways to God. Such growth does not happen overnight, but we notice changes. Most of us are not ready to lay down our lives for others, but as we grow in Christ, we are able to care for others more—that is, we may be able to be kinder, more generous, even sacrificial, to others. We may find it easier to pray too. People who have always gotten on our last nerve may become easier to take. Eventually we may even feel love for them. If God's love is infinite, we should be able to grow in love, if we lean on God to teach us. Maturing in love moves us toward the love Jesus has for us. Jesus directed the disciples to deeper love only after they walked with him several years. Growth takes time.

As you open your journal, think about your ability to love. Can you think of a time you were able to care about someone you didn't know you could care about? Are there ways your Christian life is bearing fruit in the world? Take a moment to remember Lent last year. What were you like? Has your faith expanded in the year? What practice have you taken on to help you discover new life in Christ? Take time to consider each question. Record your answers and see what God is doing through you and in you.

Prayer: *Lamb of God, you give everything for us. Teach us to love more and more. Amen.*

32[d] Day of Lent (Saturday) Numbers 21:4–9

"And we detest this miserable food."

A pastor once shared an ancient story about birds at the dawn of creation lumbering around on the ground, fretting about the annoyance their heavy arm-things were. "Why don't we have beautiful long front legs for running like gazelles do? Or strong arms for moving through trees like monkeys do?" they complained. "Instead we have these useless flappy arms." God had already given them everything they needed to soar in life, but they hadn't learned to use their gift of wings. We too waste time complaining about burdens in our life, often without noticing what God has already provided for us. Like the freed Hebrews, we gripe about whatever new circumstance we find ourselves in, without reflecting on whence we have come and where we might be headed. Although we should not depend on some talisman, like the serpent on a stake, to save us, we can benefit from determining what we have and whether God may in fact be leading us to a promised land. The Hebrews complained, yet LORD Yahweh provided everything they needed. They said they had no food, but they had daily manna—as much as they needed. They had eaten quail; God gave them victory over other peoples; they were divinely led and sheltered, month after month.

Can you note a time you complained about a situation, unable to see where God was at work? Did you eventually discover new life came from it? Can you imagine where God is leading you now?

Prayer: *God of our ancestors, thank you for faithfully providing for humanity through the millennia. Help me remember you also provide for me every day. Amen.*

Week 5: Significant Changes Happen

33^d Day of Lent (Sunday) John 12:20–33

"Sir, we wish to see Jesus."

Many scholars lean toward the opinion that the people asking to see Jesus were not Jewish. A Gentile request would be shocking. Philip was so flummoxed, he checked it out with Andrew before approaching Jesus. Opening the good news to Gentiles is an extraordinary change. Like a grain of wheat appearing to die so it will bear fruit, the message of Jesus is facing a dramatic new juncture, so much so that even the divine voice is raised. What would it mean to share God's love with Gentiles? At the same time, Jesus realizes his hour has come; his arrival in Jerusalem introduces the conclusion of his earthly ministry (and life).

Do you think Jesus sees himself as the grain of wheat? Some seeds fall to the ground and actually do die. Other seeds germinate and sprout, promising tremendous change and fruit resulting. When it comes to a seed, or the hearing of the message of Jesus, it can either actually lie there and do nothing, or it can be willing to change dramatically, sprout, grow, become life-giving, bearing fruit for the nourishment of many. This is more than changing hairstyles; it reveals more and more clearly that Jesus is Savior of the world. Can you write about other changes in Jesus' life? Someone taught him to speak. To do carpentry. To read scripture and apply it to life. Are some changes more significant than others? How might his understanding of God's will for the world have changed through the years?

Prayer: *Self-giving Savior, throughout your brief life you changed and grew. Help me not be afraid of change in my faith. Amen.*

34th Day of Lent (Monday)

Leviticus 20:22–26 and
Jeremiah 10:1–5

"Do not learn the way of the nations."

Throughout history, groups separated themselves from other people. Sometimes we claim the "others" are too primitive to understand our ways. We are embarrassed to remember that our history reveals people have claimed some "others" are subhuman, so it doesn't matter what we do to them. Their lives are treated as if they have no value. Such attitudes are why many Christians feel the need to state that "black lives matter," because our society often acts as if black lives do not matter. We don't say they matter more, but they must matter equally. Some groups argue that people of "other" religions are heathens who do not understand God, so we must keep separate to stay pure. Places in the Bible also indicate the "chosen" must keep separate from "others." Nations that inhabited the land the Hebrews traveled through were considered unclean, as certain animals were. The worship practices of these "others" were considered worthless. God's special people were to keep themselves pure. Our focus this week is on the assurance that change happens. We are invited to notice that even what is written in scripture may be reinterpreted or altered by other scripture.

Can you remember a time you were told to keep away from another kind of person? Can you remember a time someone wanted to keep separate from you? Journal those two memories. How do such distinctions make you feel now? How does it feel that some directions for separations are even in scripture? Do you think God intends for us to draw such distinctions?

Prayer: *Creator of all peoples, help us understand how separations hurt us. Amen.*

35th Day of Lent (Tuesday) Deuteronomy 5:12–15

"Or the resident alien in your towns, so that your male and female slaves may rest as well as you."

In light of yesterday's readings, we see clearly that Hebrew Scripture does not speak with a singular voice about keeping separate from the uncleanness of "others." Thank goodness. Here, in the Ten Commandments, we are told the foreigners living among the Hebrew people should share Sabbath rest. The text indicates enslaved Gentiles are living among the chosen people. Obviously, they are not wholly separated from each other. Gentiles are described as living among the people; they are workers with members of Hebrew families, so they too must follow the commandment. They too deserve Sabbath rest. In considering the situation, Hebrews are to remember their own enslavement and treat Gentiles equitably. It would not be right for the Hebrew families to have a day of rest but not the Gentile families living among them. God has commanded a day of Sabbath rest. Even Gentiles must obey.

Write out your thoughts about how scripture seems to say both that people need to stay separate and that they may live and work together. Do you think God's mind changed about clean and unclean? Might the people who wrote down these ancient stories have had different opinions about interactions between peoples? Did you ever change your attitude toward a person different from you? Perhaps someone whose English was not fluent, or someone whose orientation was different from yours or whose ethnicity was different? Think through and chronicle how the change happened. Was God at work when you opened yourself to people not like you?

Prayer: *Amazing Trinity, guide me to understand that since every person is created in your image, no one is "other." Amen.*

36th Day of Lent (Wednesday) Matthew 10:1–8

"Go nowhere among the Gentiles, and enter no town of the Samaritans."

Even Jesus is influenced by scripture and the religious traditions around him. He sends out his friends to preach the good news of God's love and to heal all manner of ailments without expecting payment, but with a blunt restriction. They must not go among Gentiles or enter Samaritan towns. Jesus says the word of God's realm is for the people of Israel. Only Jews receive healing from those who are sent out. We might understand a parent making sure her children alone are fed if there is famine in the land and she has only a small amount of food, but Jesus seems to have an infinite supply of healing power. If so, then he appears stingy with healings and sharing the good news of God's realm. After all, if the disciples share wholeness and the gospel with a group of non-Jews, isn't there still plenty left for the Jews?

What do you think? Is it disturbing to think of Jesus not wanting to share the good news with "others"? Write your thoughts. Are you inclined to find an excuse for him or explain away his prejudice? Might this help us remember Jesus is not only divine—he is also human? Have you ever experienced a group that seemed stingy with the gospel, perhaps a congregation that claims to welcome all but seems to exclude some? Have you ever been stingy with the healing good news by remaining quiet when someone around you might have appreciated knowing Jesus loves them?

Prayer: *Blessed Jesus, you are incarnate Word and son of Mary. Like each of us, you were influenced by traditions. Help us understand you. Amen.*

37th Day of Lent (Thursday)

Matthew 15:21–28

"Yes, Lord, yet even the dogs eat the crumbs that fall from their masters' table."

Did you notice? Jesus used the exact same phrase he used when he sent out the Twelve. His message is for the lost sheep of the house of Israel. Non-Jews are excluded from hearing the words of life. A little over a year ago, a church group went out to lunch after their ladies' Bible study concluded. One of the topics they discussed while they waited for their food was evil. Is there a personified devil, or is there only evil which happens in nature and by human weakness? They expressed differing opinions. All had been Christians for some years, yet they agreed they were still learning, so their differences were okay with them. If even Jesus could apparently learn and grow in his faith, these women could be comfortable with their varying opinions. The Canaanite woman was certainly "other" to Jesus. She was Gentile and a woman—someone the Twelve would have skipped in their earlier preaching travels. But her persistence got Jesus to listen, and even to grant her request. They talked and listened to each other, and Jesus was willing to make a change in his own understanding of God's will for the world.

Did you consider before how Jesus had to make changes in his beliefs, even in something as basic as the separation of Jews and Gentiles? In your journal, reflect on some faith issue you matured on, some position on which you changed. Did you realize your theology changed? How did it happen? Was it difficult?

Prayer: *Jesus, priceless Treasure, thank you for modeling growth and change for us, so we too can grow and change in our faith. Amen.*

38th Day of Lent (Friday) Acts 10

"So Peter invited them in and gave them lodging."

This memorable narrative about Cornelius and Peter is a crucial step on the developmental journey of early Christianity. Cornelius was not Jewish, and Peter was fastidiously Jewish. Peter probably never even allowed a Gentile's shadow to fall on him, much less entered someone's home. Surely he never imagined eating and sleeping in one. Cornelius was amazingly open to hearing the good news of God's love manifest through Jesus of Nazareth; and Peter was amazingly open to how God continues to reveal divine truths. Why is this crucial for us? Most Christians do not have Jewish ancestry, so for us to become followers of Jesus Christ, the people of the Way had to open the doors of faith to Gentiles (us). Think what a change Peter went through. His vision allowed him to welcome Gentile "others" into his home as guests, then accompany them to a Gentile's home and even to go in. We should be very grateful. Peter trusted his vision even though it refuted what scripture and tradition stated clearly.

Might this be a lesson for today? Have you ever been led to interpret a passage of scripture or a Christian tradition differently? Write about the experience. Did the change in your understanding make your faith feel larger or smaller? Might God be inviting you to stretch and grow again somehow in your interpretation of the faith? Most of us feel pretty locked into what we believe. Can you be as brave as Peter was if God leads?

Prayer: *How are you stretching me in my faith, wondrous Sovereign of the universe? Amen.*

39th Day of Lent (Saturday)

Romans 5:1–11 and Galatians 3:28

"While we were enemies, we were reconciled to God through the death of his Son."

This passage in Romans says it bluntly: We were reconciled to God while we were still God's enemies. Isn't that amazing? People rarely quote this part of Romans, but it is a stark statement. God justifies us; we do nothing. Paul says it in various ways. It's always God's grace that reaches down wherever we are and rescues us in spite of ourselves. While we are still sinning, ignoring God completely, grace gets poured all over us. Christ gives his life to show God's love. What a glorious, holy gift! But let's face what that means. We are saved while we are "other." Our joyous response to God's grace might be to become followers of Jesus Christ, but we are not "saved" because we are Christian. Paul states people are reconciled to God while they are still God's enemies; the enemies are reconciled. This applies to everyone. Since people do nothing to earn grace, no one is outside that grace. In other words, there are no longer any "others," because Christ came for the world.

Can you chronicle your thoughts about every person being reconciled while they are yet sinners? What does it mean that there is no longer Jew or non-Jew, male and female? Write out your own story of salvation. Do you remember when you first realized you had been reconciled to God, forgiven of your sins, saved? How does that feel? Are you willing to be generous and share your story with someone else?

Prayer: *Savior of the world, thank you for including even me in your salvation, for I was certainly "other" than you. Amen.*

Week 6: What About Holy Week?

40th Day of Lent (Sunday)

Mark 11:1–11

"You will find tied there a colt that has never been ridden."

Lots of our congregations celebrate Palm Sunday today. Others observe this as the Sunday of Palms and Passion. These churches hear much of the passion narrative in worship today, so congregants do not shout "hosanna!" today and then lose themselves in regular life during the week until Sunday rolls around again and they arrive shouting "alleluia!" There is a lot of agony between hosanna and alleluia. For our week, we will deliberately travel with Jesus each day, so let's focus just on the palm procession today, which Jesus clearly controls. People give him a hero's welcome as he rides humbly into Jerusalem. Crowds cheer him as one who comes in God's name. They anticipate the return of David's lineage to the throne. But those who first heard Mark's account and those of us hearing it today know that Jesus rides into Jerusalem in the shadow of the cross. Can you feel it? Then, as if he is checking to make sure all the pieces are in place for the next stage of his journey, he looks around in the temple before retiring to Bethany. We can almost hear the air crackling with anticipation. We almost hold our breath, feeling something is about to split wide open. Although Jesus has arrived in Jerusalem, the journey is not yet complete.

Record your thoughts as Holy Week begins. Do you have memories of past Holy Weeks? Are they about bonnets or meals, or do they focus on the journey Jesus continues to take?

Prayer: *Blessed are you, child of David's line, continuing your journey. As Holy Week begins, give me the strength to keep holding your hand. Amen.*

41st Day of Lent (Monday) Mark 14:3–10

"What she has done will be told in remembrance of her."

Throughout history, women have been caregivers during life changes. They give birth; they teach children basic religious lessons; they nurse family during illness and prepare bodies after death. If we look around most congregations, women outnumber men. They have been significant caretakers of the Christian faith for two millennia. At the same time, women are minimized, forgotten, or neglected in scripture and in Christian tradition. Here, in the story where one disciple betrays, another denies, the closest fall asleep, and all the men eventually run away, we should notice that this female follower, whose name has been forgotten, recognizes who Jesus is. He is God's chosen one, and according to Hebrew Scripture, he is to be anointed. She tends to him. Her actions acknowledge that Jesus is Messiah, the Christ, the Anointed One. Jesus predicts she will be remembered wherever the good news is proclaimed, yet we often ignore her. So, let us celebrate her today. Facing the coming brutality and torture, Jesus is comforted by this one disciple, who honors him, pouring out extravagant loving care.

Can you remember a time in your life someone recognized you were in pain, or afraid of what was ahead, or brokenhearted? How did they show care for you? How did their care feel? Could you write them a note of appreciation and mail it? As you consider what lies ahead for Jesus, can you write to him in your journal describing how you would like to care for him as the cross looms?

Prayer: *Anointed One of God, you are Monarch of the universe, yet you prepared to give yourself over to our worst tendencies. You are Love Amazing. Amen.*

42d Day of Lent (Tuesday) Isaiah 49:1–7

"I will give you as a light to the nations."

This is scripture Jesus grew up hearing, yet he would not have anticipated that millennia later some people would identify him with God's Servant. Many scholars believe the writers meant Israel as God's chosen Servant; others argue the passage can still be used to help us understand Jesus. No wonder the interpretation today is mixed, since Isaiah paints a mixed portrait. The Servant appears to be an abject failure, yet God promises to be glorified through him. Even when the Servant senses complete futility, LORD Yahweh says merely reconciling unfaithful Israel back to God is not enough. Instead, the Servant will have a more monumental task, namely illuminating God's salvation for all nations. Rulers to the ends of the world will acknowledge the Servant as God's chosen one. Certainly during Holy Week, we sense the reality of Jesus' apparent failure, even as we acknowledge him as Savior of the world.

What about your own life of faith? Have you ever felt the failure of some important ministry or mission you believed God was guiding you to perform? Write out some experience you have had of trying to serve God. If you cannot remember a time you felt you failed in a mission, might that mean you have not been bold enough in stepping out to try something new? Considering what you know about the radical teachings of Jesus, is there a project you could introduce in your congregation that would be a gift to those in need in the world?

Prayer: *Chosen Servant of God, we remember your struggles this week. We honor you as our teacher and Savior. Guide us to carry on your ministry. Amen.*

43[d] Day of Lent (Wednesday) Mark 14:12–25

"Make preparations for us there."

Jesus is in control here just as he was on Palm Sunday. He has already set preparations in motion. Everything is as he predicted, including the room, "furnished and ready." This may be where we want to slip our hand out of Jesus' hand, because no one really wants to go where we know this is headed. Yet, before the crushing events we know are coming, Jesus carves out this treasured time together, so we actually want to be there too. Granted, he predicts betrayal, but we also sense the intimacy of the passover meal shared among closest friends. These who shared everything month after month will share this precious meal of remembrance of God's freeing the people from enslavement. They will eat from the same plate, dip unleavened bread together into the main dish, probably drink from the same cup, and sing together. Jesus will inform them that this is their last precious meal together. Any perceptive listeners to this story will sense their tiny shelter of calm is about to be split open by the powers of hell.

Do you sense divine love filling the upper room? Can you feel Jesus surrounding the little band of followers with holy safety? Then, can you sense the week's tension rising around them? You know the story, although you will benefit from reading pieces again, day by day. Did something new for your journey strike you in today's reading? Be especially careful to write down things you may want to remember later.

Prayer: *Lamb of God, your love for us never fails, no matter how much we fail you. Let me sense a time of protected calm with you this night. Amen.*

44th Day of Lent (Thursday) John 14:18–29

"I will not leave you orphaned."

Each gospel shows differing details of the Last Supper, but each is charged with power and emotion. Jesus always controls the situation. Here in John, he informs the disciples that he will be executed, but they do not need to panic. Their heavenly Parent will not leave them as orphaned children. The Advocate, the Holy Spirit will come among them and strengthen them in the faith. They will be able to recall Jesus' teachings; they will learn new teachings from the Spirit; and they will be at peace and unafraid. You can almost hear Jesus tell them, "It feels scary, but we've got you." Does it seem strange that Jesus urges them to rejoice that he is returning to the heavenly Parent, the One he calls Abba? Isn't it amazing that as Jesus faces torturous death, his major concern is comforting his followers? He understands how terrified they are that he plans to leave them soon. His death flies in the face of everything they have come to believe about him.

Can you remember a time you felt nervous or afraid of some change that was coming? Did you remember that God promised not to abandon you? Have you ever felt God's arms holding you in a difficult situation? Have you ever asked God to fill you with calm assurance? You might write about it in your journal. Do you know someone who would benefit from your reminding them of God's unfailing presence with them now? How might you approach them?

Prayer: *Loving God, you are Creator, Christ, and Holy Spirit. I offer thanks and praise for your constant presence in my life. Amen.*

45th Day of Lent (Friday)

Mark 14:32—15:39

"Enough! The hour has come."

Take your time reading the scripture. No need to rush. Then you may want to sit quietly, digesting the scene. In your journal, you could list the different people who appear in this reading. Is there a person or two you identify with? What it is about them that is familiar to you? Or you might want to list the different titles people use to identify Jesus. I think there are at least eight. Does the title a person uses for Jesus indicate something about their relationship with him? What titles do you use for him? Why? Most importantly, you may want to reflect on your own reactions to the absolute self-giving love of God that Jesus pours out on the world during his last hours of life. Do you want to write about it? You have accompanied Jesus all the way to Jerusalem and the cross. How does that feel?

Prayer: *Crucified Lord, open my mind to understand your sacrifice and open my heart to love you more. Amen.*

46th Day of Lent (Saturday) Mark 15:40–47

"He then rolled a stone against the door of the tomb."

Pastors often spend Holy Saturday already deep into their Easter preparations mindset. They make sure that the lilies are arranged correctly, that the sermon speaks to the "regulars" as well as those who haven't entered the church since Christmas. Last year, I was briefly between pastoral calls, so I had no Easter worship preparations to arrange. Thus, I spent Holy Saturday fully sensing the cold, dead stone blocking the entrance to the tomb. It was a wonderful gift. At the same time, it was awful. Covid-19 had practically everyone secluded across the country. Jesus' words "it is finished" kept echoing in my head. All done. Nothing more. Holy Saturday was a day of empty waiting, staring alone into the post-crucifixion abyss. I kept thinking of the women whose lives were filled with purpose as they provided for Jesus in Galilee. They too were disciples, faithful followers, except they didn't desert him as the males had. Society had relegated them to the periphery, but they stayed; they looked on from the required distance; and they saw where the body was laid. And then, they too spent this awful day staring at the post-crucifixion abyss in their lives.

Do you sense an emptiness where you felt Jesus' hand in yours over the past six weeks? Today might be a good occasion to reread your Lenten journal. What ideas do you want to press home in your thinking? Do you recall the love Jesus Christ lavished on you? How will you respond to him?

Prayer: *Blessed Savior, beyond my understanding, you gave yourself over to our worst. Amazing love poured on me. I miss your hand in mine. Amen.*

47th Day of Lent (Easter Vigil) — Mark 16:1–8

"So they went out and fled from the tomb, for terror and amazement had seized them."

The Easter Vigil often begins in darkness, outside, where a fire is kindled. The leader proclaims that this night the Crucified One crossed from death to life. The lighted Christ candle then moves the congregation inside. The service proceeds in relative darkness as Hebrew Scriptures trace the story of humankind, God choosing Abraham's line, the Hebrew people's release from enslavement, and the prophetic promises of wholeness and salvation in God's realm for all. Then, following the renewal of baptismal commitments, the sanctuary explodes with lights. Drapings are removed from the altar. Easter lilies are uncovered so their aroma permeates the space. Music begins at full volume, and the proclamation is boldly made: "Alleluia! Christ is risen!" This glorious service makes clear that death cannot have the last word. God's life is always victorious. Reading Mark's account of Easter may seem anticlimactic, since the women respond with shocked silence. But this passage, which scholars tell us is the gospel's original ending, strikes home. Those women knew Jesus was dead. They stayed at the cross, probably making eye contact with the suffering Savior, until his eyes closed for the last time. They knew the stone had sealed in a cold, lifeless body. So, an amazed and terrified response to the announcement of Jesus' resurrection makes perfect sense. No wonder they fled and told no one. But, of course, their silence was not permanent. The great good news exploded across the Roman Empire. The Crucified One is alive! He is risen indeed! Alleluia.

Prayer: *All praise to you, resurrected Lord. Alleluia. Amen.*

Reading 48 (Easter Sunday) John 20:1–18

"Mary Magdalene went and announced to the disciples, 'I have seen the Lord'."

On this spectacular day, we rightly set aside time to spend in private devotion. Each of us wants to experience the resurrected Christ personally, which is good. We yearn to encounter Jesus in our own garden, or kitchen, or devotional chair. But our risen Savior always sends us into community, so no wonder we discover the presence of the risen Savior best among gathered Easter worshippers, as resurrection hymns flood our being and the scent of lilies transports us to his morning garden. For many, the Easter service is the most glorious worship of the entire year. The whole congregation proclaims death is defeated. God's love wins. Together we are most likely to sense the Living Christ, to hear our Savior call our name. Even if we worship online, the power of the Holy Spirit moves among us and makes us church together. On this holy day, we realize our Lenten journey does not end in Jerusalem, but here in the spiritual presence of the Living Christ.

For today's journal entry, notice that Mary, not a man, is the first evangelist. Jesus sends an unlikely woman to announce the resurrection to the other disciples. Might Jesus be sending unlikely you to speak a word of resurrection joy to someone you know? Spend time being open to hearing what Jesus is saying to you. Write out what you would say to another person. Who needs to hear about your encounter with the risen Christ? Have you thanked Jesus for calling your name?

Prayer: *Glorious risen Christ, thank you for loving humanity no matter what. And thank you, Almighty God, for displaying the victory of your grace in the resurrected presence of Christ. Help me receive that presence in my life, today and always. Amen.*